Love
Poems
and
Other
Terrible
Problems

Love
Poems
and
Other
Terrible
Problems

Poems by

CHARLES ZEIDERS

il piccolo editions
by
fisher king press

il piccolo editions by Fisher King Enterprises LLC
www.fisherkingpress.com
info@fisherkingpress.com
+1-307-222-9575

Love Poems and Other Terrible Problems
Copyright © 2017 Charles Zeiders
ISBN: 978-1-77169-044-7 Paperback
ISBN: 978-1-77169-045-4 eBook
First Edition

Published simultaneously in Canada and the United States of America. For information on obtaining permission for use of material from this work, please submit a written request to:

permissions@fisherkingpress.com

To my love

Emily

INTRODUCTION

In my mind's eye, an orthodox Christian poet resembles a tweedy, pale, bespectacled figure sitting in a plush armchair by a lit fireplace discussing medieval poetry (like the Inklings). In this book, *Love Poems and Other Terrible Problems*, the orthodox Anglo-Catholic poet, Charles Zeiders, shatters my stereotyped vision.

Zeiders writes poems that are as profane and earthbound as they are spiritual. At times, the verse is lovely and limpid ("We walk into a forest of birch and pine. A dove flutters ahead of us to the forgotten spring"). The opening poem, "A description of things in the tradition of Walt Whitman," describes an epiphanic moment with a timeless grace:

> From the arctic orb
> A moon man looks down
> And studies me where I stand…
>
> The dark creeps from the west and north, and a singular cold
> Oppresses the place.

Yet, in the same poem, the epiphanic moment devolves into present day travails as:

> Talking heads speculate militarized cops will occupy our towns…
> The hawk-faced girl from the State Department makes a scoffing noise
> Snorting that Putin threatens the integrity of NATO

Other poems are hysterical (sometimes a homonym with these poems), silly, and surreal:

> Plump, amorous Cartwright—underpants too tight.

1

No luck with Mrs. Porter.
None tonight.

Or, just as silly:

Having dreamt that Ronald McDonald is a demon, I now
Forswear Big Macs and repent French Fries.

Other poems, though, are journeys into the night: grappling with nihilism, spiritual degradation, childhood rape, and violence. He exults in the pathetic nature of the many male personas he shuffles through his poems. He revels sometimes in their humiliation and suffering. His almost willful humiliation of these personas invokes the god-forsaken, yet spiritually yearning characters in Graham Greene's novels, except Zeiders is also a first-rate comedian and satirist. One persona, Cartwright, is perhaps the most skewered persona. Here is Cartwright begging a woman for sex:

I know that you feel old
But can't you make contact
With your vanishing impulses
And kiss my lips?

Zeiders is a practicing clinical psychologist as well as a poet. He displays this psychological acumen with his portrait of a sociopathic Episcopalian-style bishop named Ladysmith-Jones and a poignant and more nuanced portrait of a poet and victim of pedophilia named Ned. With each portrait, Zeiders leads the reader into spiritual and psychological damnation. Only a transcendent awakening, spiritual love, which Ladysmith-Jones is too afflicted to find, redeems.

The poems, by contrast, to Emily, are exultant paeans to a lover. Zeiders is a poet, and no doubt a man, of strong passions

2

and enthusiasms. His intensity for his lover (who, in a poem, becomes his wife) radiates from his life-force:

> Just imagining you
>
> Causes me to burst into the air
> Fly over the alps and oceans
>
> Soar over expanses
> Fly high above war and peace
>
> Ignore the affairs of leaders in
> Small capitals below my
>
> Jetting body
> Until I land by you
>
> And love you
> And love you
> And love you

Throughout these poems, there is a longing, a wish deferred, for wholeness, unity, transcendence. Zeiders knows the past is past, that his orthodox religious faith has fully retreated (as Matthew Arnold wrote: to the breath of the night wind)--that, within academia and our intellectual Zeitgeist, he is an outsider. Another persona, Jacques Foucault, a literary theorist and academic, although cartoonish, is a triumphant deconstructionist who judges a writer's (Zeiders himself?) religiosity as: "the self-indulgent, needy aspirations of a man who cannot face within himself that life holds no guarantee of anything."

Zeiders provides no defense for this judgement. And that is one of the many strengths of these poems. He presents a complex spiritual faith that defies any stereotype a reader may have about religion. Instead, his faith is messy and sometimes impotent, inconsolable, despairing (as well as a buoy against the ignorant armies clashing in the night and a source of radiant spiritual love).

Despite Zeiders' orthodox Anglicanism, this is not a book for a conservative or a fundamentalist (although they may benefit from it). Religious faith here is a universe of complexity not certitude.

Regarding complexity, throughout these poems, Zeiders mixes street vernacular and nonsense rhymes with poetry that is spare and crystalline. He uses this gift for language to create a multi-vocal world. Maybe his experience as a psychotherapist has contributed to this, but his book, though short, contains a multitude of distinctive voices and characters. It should be noted too that there is a touching poem about Andrew Wyeth and his muse, Helga; there are short meditative poems, as well as references to Zeiders' clinical work that sometimes act as buttresses or links.

Love Poems and Other Terrible Problems teems with psychic and spiritual energy. It's like a Hieronymus Bosch painting that includes the Marx Brothers and splotches of transcendent gold. But it's more than this metaphor and perhaps any metaphor. Even this agnostic writer can delight in the beauty and craftsmanship of these poems.

Peter Devlin
Writer
Washington, D.C
January 23, 2017

PRELUDE

A description of things in the tradition of Walt Whitman

Under frozen heaven I am in a vast equanimity.

From the arctic orb
A moon man looks down
And studies me where I stand

On earth
In America
In Pennsylvania
In Bryn Mawr.

The dark creeps from the west and north, and a singular cold
Oppresses the place.

Nervous people leave lights on at all hours.
In their homes they turn up the heat.

The semester ends.
The students drink in bars on The Avenue.
They look exhausted.
The more conscientious coeds march through the streets.
On banners they write the names of citizens killed by frantic police.

Talking heads speculate militarized cops will occupy our towns.
Someone says all the grand juries are rigged.
Before his microphone is cut
A professor without a tie yells that the real issue
Is the weak dollar
And imminent currency collapse.

The hawk-faced girl from the State Department makes a scoffing noise
Snorting that Putin threatens the integrity of NATO
And ISIS possesses more militant vigor than the press reports!

A civil liberties expert
Retches out that America is a spy state
And the federal government is obliged to
Repent by upholding the Constitution while keeping us safe;
From behind sunglasses
He shouts that a just government must govern transparently.

A cloud removes itself from the moon's face
And I step into a sliver of light that touches my corner of the frozen
snow.

Authoritative voices fade and inner voices speak:

"Everything is ambiguous and you no longer fear that.
There are people left alive whom you love.
You are the man who blessed someone today.
A secret good thing occurs, but no one knows its nature."

I look up to the moon.
The man in the crater waves at me.
I wave back as he drops a silver cord to me.
Through hand gestures he invites me to climb.
He holds up a bottle of moon port, suggesting a drink.

"No thank you, kind moon man," I yell in a voice not my own.
"I think my place is here, with the ambiguity and big problems.
But thank you for your generous offer."

The moon man drops a note to me that takes
Over an hour to reach the earth and
My frozen patch of moonlit snow.
The letter lands on the tip of my boot.

It reads, "Under frozen heaven, you are in a vast equanimity."

LOVE POEMS

Emily's poem

To what shall
I compare you
When even hyperbole fails --

A gem?

Prepared by nature, gods,
HaShem?

For in you lightness
And brightness
Shine forth
With such unadulterated
Beauty

That I throw other sense
And sight away

Dream of you at night
And yearn for you by day.

A kiss epiphany at a fancy restaurant with Emily

By offering religious observations about eternity

And the nature of my love

I embarrass you.

You stiffen.

I straighten.

Impressive small talk may be my way to recover:

"Opalescence is the key to understanding Jamie Wyeth's pig painting!"

"Rare snails must surely be anti-carcinogenic! This is indubitable!"

"Complexes populate the individual unconscious, just as archetypes populate the collective!"

"I accomplish secret things for the government!"

I make flourishes with my hand.

You sigh.
Your delicate shoulders rise and fall.

The corners of your pretty lips
Turn down.
You pout.

I feel heartbroken and homesick.
But I do not care.
In that dress you look lovely.

A speck of gold paint glistens on your chin.
All day long you restored icons.

You know my reverence for your work.
You know I am an icon kisser.

You sense my religiosity masks loneliness.
And insecurity.
(Sometimes.)

You smile at my serious silence.
I am embarrassed.

But I love you,
So my embarrassment does not embarrass me.

I kiss your upturned lips.
(Suddenly!)
You kiss back.

Something happens to my heart.
I am frankly, fully, and finally consoled.

You whisper
(Your breath touches my face with sweetness)
That eternity will take care of itself.

We kiss over and over.

For me
With you
Tonight, Emily,
Now is forever
And joy.

Innocent Freudian poem

You're the pretty cashier at the grocery.
I bought bananas from you.
Then I dreamed you emerged from a lake, naked.

I thought I was dreaming my friend Tim's dream.
He's always been the lady's man.

Your eyes were amethysts,
Goddess eyes.

I had the vaguest notion
That I blurted something incomprehensible
That made you smile
And you closed the store.

You looked mischievous and pleased.

We held hands
And laughed while we walked to your flat.

Imagine my joy when I awoke and you were real,
Asking me to stay, and to purchase more bananas.

The space around her

you should have seen
the space around her

when she left
it moved to where she was not

and filled the void
like hope

You

You connect me to the farthest stars in the universe

And to the ground beneath my feet.

The water is alive and the wind will blow where it will

In the late summer evening
We embrace.

You hold a rose.
Pure white specks interrupt
Petals of blood red.

This, you say,
Signifies
Purity after our redemption.

We walk into
A forest
Of birch and pine.

A dove
Flutters ahead of us
To the forgotten spring.

We dip our fingers
Into the pool.
We touch each other's foreheads.

We see a path that leads to the ruined chapel.
We follow it.
We sense that prayer unleashes force there.
We sense that the grace of the place will
Make our souls articulate.

We sense that the One Who Listens—hears
With fierce and loving prejudice.

The altar is mossy.
We kneel.
"Turn the heart of Eve to Adam," I pray loudly.
"Turn the heart of the man to the woman,"
You pray with power.

A gust rips through the tree tops.
It stops.
The little spring trickles.

We know that our hearts have turned.

You rise.
On tiptoes you lay your rose upon the altar.
"The water is alive," you say,
"And the wind will blow where it will."

On the eve of marrying Emily

Sweetheart, I love you with all my beating heart.
Just imagining you

Causes me to burst into the air
Fly over alps and oceans

Soar over expanses
Fly high above war and peace

Ignore the affairs of leaders in
Small capitals below my

Jetting body
Until I land by you

And love you
And love you
And love you

And exult
In the unlimited discovery of your unending beauty.

How wonderful I find you!
How happy I want to make you!

How can Providence be so sweet as to plant you in my life?
What thanks I shall give when I hold you as my wife!

Seven schmi-ku

i.
Eyes meet.
Hands touch.
Worship.

ii.
She lounges naked, smiling.
Nocturnal joy.
Aerobic.

iii.
Minus pants.
Loquacious.
She inflames my heart.

iv.
A potentially fat-shaming verse lamentably placed below
Plump, amorous Cartwright—underpants too tight.
No luck with Mrs. Porter.
None tonight.

v.
After bathing,
She hums.
A masterpiece.

vi.
Nude beach.
Seven hours.
Boredom.

vii.
Napping with Emily.
Seven hours.
Paradise.

Wyeth to Helga

I paint you.
Each brushstroke constellates the primordial energy of our love.

It is visible to mystics and angels.
It is a force between us.

Our love is erotic and spiritual.
Our love is Eden and the New Jerusalem.
Our love is Brandywine and forever.

Our love is its own reason.
Our love is its own justification.
Our love is deeply personal.
Our love is inflicted upon us.

Our love binds me to this easel.
Our love binds you to that model's bench.

My tempera upon your canvas writes the wedding vows of my heart.

Our quiet process is eloquent with mutual choosing.
Yet, a Mystery chooses us together.

Outside my studio sun shines on fiddleheads,
Sycamore,
and the ancient battlefield.
But I focus on the canvas and you.

I render love meticulously.
I paint slowly.

You are quiet and naked and patient with me.
I wipe paint on my smock.
My nakedness is for later.

For now I paint.
I paint slowly.
I love your eyes.

In self-surrender I paint you a present.

In time
We will acknowledge
This painting as the legitimate child I bore you.

The sacrament of our joyful invincibility

Emily,

Fall is here.
Days shorten.
As with my life.

Orange adorns
The late afternoon sky.
As with my life.

Mortality
Is
In focus.

The media
Forecasts
Disaster.

Famine, plague, and revolution
Will break out just when
Our money runs out.

And so say the presidential candidates.
One is said to be a malignant narcissist.
The other irredeemably corrupt.
They propose to build glittering versions of the spiritually defunct polis.
Each is possessed of the spirit of Judas Iscariot.

We do not overly apprehend.
Dread eludes us.
We are hopeful.

We awoke this morning.
We drank coffee.
We felt happy.

Careless of death and uncertainty
(They weren't even in your eyes)
You kissed me.
You handed me lunch.
And you packed me off to my practice
        to heal the sick.

Your gaze and your touch
Outwardly express
That Eternity's Author

Has something rather beautiful in mind—

Like your music and your paintings
Like your singing voice
Like your compositions at noonday
Like your embrace in the night
Like your smile
And your presence
        in my life.

Here,
With you, Emily,
In the beauty of our human caring
Vouched safe by the Reign of the Heavens
Under the sovereignty of the good Prince who loves us

Is the sacrament of our joyful invincibility.

OTHER TERRIBLE PROBLEMS

Syrian dream

After the embassy closed
Washington ordered us to remain.

Objectives were ambiguous.
We wore black suits, ties, and sunglasses.

We looked the part.
Targets.

The least trained man was me.
The other guys were Special Forces.

The sounds of gunfire and Arabic came close.
Somehow I survived the firefight.

The other guys were dead.
I raised my pistol to my head.

The insurgents stood around me.
They held Kalashnikovs. Amused.

When I squeezed off the round
My hand shook so much that

I shot their leader in the face.
Gore splashed.
Without a head
He fell.

Before astonished eyes
I ran into an alley

And all the way to Turkey.

Cartwright reads about Nietzsche's demise, rejects
the crazed philosopher as a guide to ultimate value

i.

Beyond the brothels
In the ordinary part of Basel

Dwelt Nietzsche
Bedeviled as autumn

When the leaf liberates
Wildly from the wood

And flutters from end
To un-end

Adrift in currents
Preventing arrival.

It stares earthward
At destination death

Where decay
Is inevitable and ultimate.

What better reason
For the philosopher

Of Superman
To embrace

The iceman's
Flogged horse

And collapse
Into Womb Mind?

He called himself crucified.

ii.
Plump, amorous Cartwright
Lies in bed undressed.
He reads of Nietzsche, unimpressed.

"I must dismiss this dismal verse!
And blurt the truth, conviction terse!

It's Mrs. Porter, stupid!"

The narcissist in spring

Seminary classmates describe Frederick Ladysmith-Jones' student years with envy and disgust. Frederick gained notoriety as a brilliant, radically conservative theologian with no tolerance for ambiguity. Widely read and annoyingly confident, he gave no ground in theological debates. He backed his arguments with excellent points drawn from scripture, tradition, and reason. One contemporary noted:

> Fred spoke with amazing authority. He came off like some guy from *Downton Abbey* or the House of Lords. He fascinated people with brilliant linguistic skills while oozing a messianic sense of himself. Faculty and students gravitated to him; they felt they could be junior saviors with him. They gave him a lot of attention and in return he made them feel special and important. His grandiosity was infectious. It was in seminary that his charisma really heated up. The faculty fed into it, too. Fred was easily their favorite student, and he received special treatment. The seminary Dean, who went on to become *Faith Cathedral's* Bishop Augustini, began to groom Fred for a big role in the Reformed Catholic movement. What Augustini didn't get was that Fred was grooming him, too. Augustini didn't see Fred's lethal ambition and megalomania. All he saw was this brilliant high church guy who would be invaluable in the Reformed Catholic Movement and in winning the culture war.

Interestingly, the Seminary Dean was psychologically minded. Prior to receiving Holy Orders, each seminarian endured a mandatory psychological examination. Dean Augustini consulted regularly with Dr. Roosevelt, the Seminary Psychologist, and generally followed the expert's recommendations.

Dr. Roosevelt administered a battery of standard psychological assessments to priest candidate Ladysmith-Jones. On a well-respected test of character pathology, Ladysmith-Jones scored positive for Narcissistic Personality Disorder and evidenced elevations on a scale of antisocial or criminal traits. Dr. Roosevelt also determined that Frederick suffered from a latent mood disorder (plus trauma and shame) that he defended against with pathological grandiosity.

Interviewed for this document, Dr. Roosevelt disclosed the following:

> Until I tested Ladysmith-Jones, Dean Augustini and I enjoyed an excellent working relationship. I figured that I'd just tell the Dean that—while brilliant—Frederick really should not be a priest. He tested out as a narcissist, and his clinical presentation supported that. His grandiosity was more pronounced than any I'd ever encountered. So I compared the way he presented with the diagnostic criteria for Narcissistic Personality Disorder. He had fantasies about becoming a historically important church figure and saving the Western world from spiritual death. He disclosed that Providence had chosen him for this great role during a high school mystical experience. Ladysmith-Jones presented as an exaggeratedly self-important young man, preoccupied with fantasies of unlimited success. He indicated that he could only be understood by other culturally and spiritually elite people. He threw the words "high church" and "Anglo-Catholic" around a lot. He was obviously put off that I was not buying into his greatness and providing him with excessive admiration. He made some dismissive remarks about psychology not really being a science. He got under my skin, and I lost my cool, which is rare for me. His sense of entitlement was unreasonable, and he had a reputation for being interpersonally exploitive. The guy was haughty.

Dr. Roosevelt informed Dean Augustini that Frederick's character pathology made him a poor priest candidate. Roosevelt expressed further concerns that Frederick's spirituality was likely to involve *de facto* self-worship, that he had the personality of a cult leader, and that he had criminal tendencies. Dr. Roosevelt presciently observed that Frederick presented a suicide risk if the "narcissistic supplies that keep his grandiosity charged up over his hidden depression were ever to be interrupted." Sadly, Augustini simply did not believe Dr. Roosevelt, who went on to observe that

> Augustini was childless, and I think he had deeply paternal feelings toward Ladysmith-Jones. He just could not abide my psychological determination about Fred's psychopathology. No father wants to hear that his son is a malignant narcissist. When Augustini told me he would put Ladysmith-Jones forward for ordination, I flipped and went over Augustini's head to the Seminary Board. Ladysmith-Jones was an impaired professional in the making and an obviously bad choice for a church leader. He also represented a threat in the making to the credibility of the Reformed Catholic Movement. Frederick had an ability to develop a theory of mind about any person who was useful to him. He lacked real empathy, but he could read people. This made him a master manipulator. Despite my efforts, he convinced the Seminary Board that he was as pure as the driven snow. With that fake English accent, he piously announced that I was an apparently well-meaning psychologist, deleteriously enlisting the tools of so-called social science upon a population of holy people called to religious life. He asked the Board if they valued the instruments of nasty secular humanism over the still, small voice that

guides the hearts of men to become priests, etc., etc. The Board got all worked up. They fired me. And Ladysmith-Jones went on to ordination.[1]

---

1 Excerpted from Charles Zeiders (2016). A 'psychological autopsy' of a malignant narcissist in church leadership: a composite scenario with discussion. *Journal of Christian Healing*, 3 (1), pp. 1 - 29.

The bad shepherd (Cartwright's first lament)

i.

Our conclusion echoes with inconclusive sadness and anger.
You promised just enough to keep me in the dysfunctional
organization. You offered friendship, camaraderie, and under-
standing. I wanted love but settled. If we did the right thing,
you said, everything would get better. By denying my desire
I already set myself on the wrong course. You disappointed
several men. You destroyed three. I will not confuse piety with
vain eroticism again. Sublimation is a sucker's game.

ii.

Allah is Allah
But a buck's a buck.
Virtue subverts
If a fuck ain't a fuck.

iii.

Mrs. Porter took offense.
"I find that Cartwright's too intense.
Still, I will not be appalled.
I must forgive that Cartwright's flawed."

Cold (Cartwright's second lament)

"I left the seminar.
The weather turned cold.
I hate the cold.
But I loved that I would see you.

We met at the bar.
It had been over twenty years.
We both looked great.
We laughed.

You ordered Champagne.
This was an excellent sign.

We talked about our college days.
You detailed your divorce.
You mentioned medical problems and menopause.
To me you were really cute.
I said it truthfully.
You were really cute.

You asked me why I never married.
"Never married, never divorced," I said.
You laughed.
I felt clever.

You told me that you did not think the night would be a date.
You smiled sweetly and told me that you reassessed.
It was all very official.
This was now a real date, et cetera, et cetera.

We drank more Champagne.

Somehow we ended up in the subway.
We were very animated and talked about something funny.
We took the Lindenwold line from Center City.

You said something about not having high expectations.
You became nervous.
I became nervous too.
I had forgotten my boner medications.

Magically, we were at your house.
We spent an inordinate amount of time with your dog Shadow.
We patted the hound and gushed over him.
We were nervous.

Even though we wanted to make love,
We were afraid to make love.

You led me to your room.
In soft light we partially stripped and climbed into your bed.
At first we were very sweet.
I enjoyed kissing you.
You seemed to enjoy kissing me.

I got a wonderful erection.
In my heart, I elated.
'Take that you hardened arteries!
Take that you bastards of high blood pressure!
This woman en-boners me!
Cupping her breast I am cured of all ailments.
Coital magnificence will be ours, you sweetie!'

You pulled back just slightly.
Second thoughts plagued you.
You do not lubricate like you used to, you said.
Menopause has taken a toll, you said.

You alluded to medical issues I simply did not understand.

My confidence and joy were in critical condition.

You told me you were not ready to take a lover so close to your divorce.
You reiterated vague mid-life sexual worries.

I rolled off you.
I un-cupped your breast.
I pulled on my underpants
We lay side by side.
We tried to sleep.

I was inflamed with lust and hope.
At any moment you would come to your senses
And we would make love.

But we did not make love.
We lay there.

Sensing my frustration you called me a cab.
You negotiated with the dispatcher.
You saved me thirty dollars.

The cab arrived.
I walked into the cold.
You told me how sorry you were.
I walked into the cold.
You told me that you would call me.
I walked into the cold.
It was quarter to four on a Sunday morning.
It was November.
The ride home was endless.
The world was dying.
It was so cold.

Drunken proposal from a short man to a hot tall woman with dismaying common sense (Cartwright entreats Mrs. Porter)

I know that you feel old
But can't you make contact
With your vanishing impulses
And kiss my lips?

Make a forever of now.
Rebuke conscience or plow
Or whatever holds you
From kissing me more
And holding my body
In sweet, kissed adore.
Can you not lay aside
The tyranny of common sense?
Can you not smash
Your inhibiting conscience
Upon a rock of real
Or concocted desire?

I'll pour the drinks.

Can you not stroke
With tender abandon
The face
That smiles at you
With unqualified desire and love?

(Is your libido underfunded?
Baby, I'll write the grant.)

Can you not assent
That it is excellent
That I might maneuver
The strings
Of that dress till you're naked?

Can you not
Upon this ridiculous soil
Give up your worries
Of Popeye and Olive Oyl?
Me too small and you too tall?
Reclining together equalizes height!

Hell, can you not for once
Just say "yes" to an obviously
Bad idea
And flee with me
To Venice?

ii.
Having exhausted himself from the afore-written ejaculation,
plump, amorous Cartwright collapsed into his pasta intoxi-
cated, while Mrs. Porter pretended not to notice and excused
herself to the toilet with consternation and graceful poise.

Strange correspondence

i.

Dear Sarah Sue Wong,

Having dreamt that Ronald McDonald is a demon, I now forswear Big Macs and repent of French fries.

Christopher Freud

ii.

Dear Sarah Sue Wong,

I understand that Christopher Freud recently e-mailed you with correspondence that demonstrates glibness for a man recently graced by God with a holy dream that revealed that the Vedic Meditation with which he once nourished his soul amounted to nothing more than spiritual junk food.

Freud writes to you in this way, dear Sarah, because he feels ashamed for you to see the utter famine within his soul. The idea that you might see his inner littleness, his tiny emaciated dehydrated loveless inner boy, so fills him with self-loathing and humiliation that he erects a shabby barrier of off-handed narcissism between himself and you.

Moreover, by minimizing the tremendous poverty of his spirit, he hides from himself and degrades the revelation that God has given him. Freud's renunciation of Vedic Meditation amounts to renouncing the very work of the Devil, a project vastly more serious than divesting emotional energy from a junk food clown.

I worry for Freud, because his shame may keep him from authentic dialogue with God. Freud's narcissistic defenses against his experience of soul-level decrepitude and inner poverty are so well developed that he may attempt to "act big" even to the One beside Whom he is appropriately small.

As Ever,

Dr. Zingfeld

iii.
Freud's Re-write of Psalm 88, accidentally left in Dr. Zingfeld's office

When nightmares tear me from sleep,
let my screams be prayers.

Misery inundates me.

Like an anorexic girl with purging behaviors
my strength floats in the toilet.

I'm blown apart.
You've abandoned me, God.

You chain me in a seaside tomb
and crash waves of your contempt over me.

You drive off my friends.
My nearness sickens them.
It sickens me, too.
My eyes ache,
because I cry all the time.

I'm dying,
but I don't think that my corpse
        will make a good impression in terms of con-
        verting others to You.

Corpses don't market the idea that You are reliable
In moments of existential torment.

I respectfully point out
that others might be more impressed
if you saved me,
even from myself.

                    Whaddya say?

iv.
Newsflash from a theologian

All close relationships hit a few bumps in the road.

Christopher Freud's friend Narcissus discerns himself into physical inactivity

Upon exposure to books
He took to thinking,

And after his marriage
This practice evolved beyond itself

Into a dream
Where all the world

Became his extension;
His gaze brought whole fields of wheat into glory

And his eye, approving,
Lent beauty to the autumn hills

Beyond the valley;
People were either this or that,

A taste he did or did not like;
His friends became hollow protagonists

Within whom his identity echoed
During dramas of his own devising;

Even his love for his wife depended
Upon his most recent insight

Or how she smelled.

At last, discerning that he was
All in All, he

Dispensed with humans altogether,
Preferring to manifest himself

From a chair
While ticking as a French clock on the mantel

Or growing in fragrant beds
Along moist rows of his madness.

Christopher Freud's anti-intellectual Blake dream, which was scary enough to cause the proud abstract thinker to scurry away from applying the dream specifically to himself, consisted of the following hypnopompic recitation

"The carpenter who bled and groaned
Reigns within my heart enthroned;

It's he who rips my schemes in half
And does so with his Father's staff.
He leads me through the valley dead
And smashes hubris on my head.

He prods my brain and says, 'Relief
Emerges from your heart's belief.'

Our God destroyed my ego's game
And so his image could reclaim.
I pushed with thought but my Lord shoved.
Sometimes it hurts to be so loved."

And Freud, who slept the unsound sleep of intellectuals, awoke shaken to derive an unflattering truth about himself, yet proceeded to depersonalize it via the following private catechism:

"My dark intellect has never really loved the Light
And could never actually stand it,
But likes to read about it
In encyclopedias."

Christopher Freud's weird prophetic vision

In the shadow of a building condemned to make room
for a structure designed to bring its owners more profit,
the Lost Art of Definitive Statements cried out,

"New concepts antiquate me. I am out of business.
As soon as my paradigms put forth their painstakingly
structured metaphors for truth, Mr. Relativity jumps out of
his absurd condominium and produces his snakeskin bag
of tricks that was purchased with humanitarian aid loaned
forth by the guilt-ridden sons of hawk-faced Calvinists.

O miserable sack! O tote bag stuffed with the accouterments
of the theological welfare state! I lament the day that your
contents were conceived when the Purely Material Corporation
produced you by digesting the truth of Spirit in vats of
the Devil's stomach acid.

Now Commercial Culture has as much philosophical validity as
Christianity
while the Whore of Totally Narcissistic Practices bares her
tattooed breasts to the taxed public who read her nipples thusly:

'Self-Validation is the idiot savant who determines how man ought
to live.
Pure Relativity renders me as valid as any corpse swinging on
a tree or any tomb empty or otherwise. Bet your boots that I am
as bad or as good as anything Christian and even better, because
I require
no repentance, and I ask no compensation for my services.
Come couple with this whore for free.'"

(Freud beheld the vision and compiled extensive mental notes. Upon the fading of the thing Freud was silent for a very long time, then sought out the physician Zingfeld for a drink.)

Atonement

With sexual slowness
She turns the waiting blade
Down
Past invisible blond hair
And into
The helpless, tense flesh.

She cuts.

Blood oozes obediently
And for the moment,
Just for the moment,
Her sin of being
Has been atoned.

Failed professor's coat

The coat
which Prof. has worn,
now shed like wool
from a sheep oft shorn,

embodied the secret agency
that crept into North America
through the cracks
despoiling the Academy
of thousands of sacks
of belief and doctrine

and, unannoyed
with the void,
proclaimed assertion of truth
as truth is seen
a laughable project
antique and mean

and an idiot wind
blowing death-oxide to tenure hopes.

An expensive coat
whose meanings suggest
that a God or Word
is a fictive guest,

that meaning derives
not from Meaning
and that truth explodes
amid its gleaning

is a coat of men under ground.

Once buttoned
from bottom to throat
the garment is Prof.'s
discredited, castaway coat

leaving him naked
unsuccessful
broke
and full of furious faith.

Christopher Freud beholds Quaker Andrew's winter of spirit

By the ancient Friends Meeting
Quaker Andrew tells us
That his spirit

Fled the stone building
And the comfort of its colonial familiarity.
Over the floor
Stained with Hessian blood
His spiritual body
In octogenarian form

Carried a burden of imminent death
To a nearby field
And collapsed

Like an oak king
Worn by a last winter.
For months snow

Covered and uncovered
Blemishes on his face.
His dreamed body froze

And a wind of needles
Punished its extremities.

Something flickered
Around his incorporeal corpse
While darkness
Overcame dismal browns

And extinguished hope
In lifeless gullies.

The land was arctic,
Full of absence,
And he was part of it.

"When I pray,"
Said Andrew,
"I pray for spring.
God's touch quickens

Dead earth
So that every crocus
Testifies to the resurrection.

Each year
Our Lord does what he does
So I don't ask
For abundant changes
In His pleasure.

Instead I pretend
(Because pretending accelerates prayer)

That it's March
And that the snow
Is melting.

I see my formerly dead spirit
Stir in the snow.

It reaches between
Its legs and smiles."

Sarah Sue Wong to Christopher Freud

Imagination keeps you
From the true experience of woman.

You suffer in the gap
Between your idea of love
And the reality of her—
    amid mutual fallenness.

When you dream,
A fantasy angel serves you.
When you awake,
A fallen man
Blinks at a dangerously dimensional woman.

Sin has a price
And virtue exacts the same.
I embody both.
Will you enter in?

A devastating blow to Mr. Writer Guy's spiritual and literary confidence

i.

From a literary materialist

Dear Mr. Writer Guy,

Besides yourself, who are you trying to kid with your whining about Post-Modernism?

You whine that it's a terrible thing not to have a sturdy metaphysic behind the written word. But if some Super Transcendent inhered within the printed document, your over-hyped Holy Writ would not have undergone two thousand years of hermeneutic analysis. The very fact that hundreds of monks, biblical scholars, and pitiful pious folks continue to develop a vast plurality of competing, yea conflicting, interpretations leads the intellectually honest mind to conclude that no one really knows what the Bible, let alone your precious (and not very effective) verse, actually denotes.

Furthermore, your own poetry shamelessly draws upon the central tenet of post-modern literary criticism, while claiming to denounce it.

Your scrapbook technique of splicing and pasting rips-off the visionary aesthetic of fragmentation inherent in better poets' structural and thematic diversity and poorly mimics the multiple schemata and decentralized texts of the internet.

Your falcon has no falconer, Mr. Writer Guy. Your attempts to marry your "writing" to a center simply cannot hold. Yours is a regressive project born from the self-indulgent, needy aspirations of a man who cannot face within himself that life holds no guarantee of anything.

God is dead, Mr. Writer Guy, along with the Unitary Self and the Text of Absolute Meaning.

Grow up and shape up, Mr. Writer Guy. God will not save you, either in life or in art, from ambiguity or difficult times.

In Truth (even though it doesn't exist),

Jacques Foucault
Emeritus Chair,
Department of Humanities without Transcendence

ii.
A Physician comforts Mr. Writer Guy

Take heart, dear boy.
Even now God saves you.
Just not on your terms.

Anything

I watch and listen.
Candy wrappers blow across the baseball diamond.
Somewhere in the distance
A dog yelps as he chokes on his chain.
In the sky migrating birds become endless clouds;
They fly to ever western sunlight in the dying sky.
Remoteness seems close.
What does anything have to do with anything?
Memories of half-formed hopes and intuitions
Float from me like easy autumn leaves.
And for the first time
I write a poem.

Physician to Patient - 1

Dear Patient,

Your present preoccupation/obsession is driving me crazy. I'm going to say it one more time:

The body is a vessel that sails us to God (and should be employed with that consideration);

In its purest form sexuality is a sacrament, not a sin;

The Song of Songs more accurately depicts the ultimate nature of the human estate than psychoanalysis.

Please memorize the above and rejoice in your incarnation.

Yours,

Doctor

Physician to Patient - 2

Dear Patient,

Let me say it this way:

Creation, of which you are a part, enjoys the Light of the Transfiguration. Some men allow this uncreated Light to apprehend and transform them. This is the light and life we have in God.

At first, it is a scary thing. Born frail and intrinsically frightened, we shrink from Love's radiant outstretching of Itself to us.

We fear passing away, like seeds into earth (I'm changing images now). But this is no death. God plants a destiny in seeds. They fall to earth to blossom.

Let the seed of your soul participate in its ripening by willingly surrendering its sovereignty to God's plan for its Becoming.

Fall to earth, dear Patient.

The Holy Trinity will nourish your soul to blossom to its intended destiny. This is your happiness. You lose nothing.

You toil in unprofitable reflection and madness.
    But toil ends.
You rage for vain understandings.
    But rage ends.
You war with literary snobs and postmodern critics.
    But war ends.
You fail at romance, friendship, and work.
    But failure ends.

Standing out of Light, you stand out of mind, out of purpose, out of success. Seeking to gain life, you lose it.

But now I commend to you the best way to live to the fullest extent.

Tumble away from your self-clinging.
Fall into the soul soil of the ever present Christ.

With this accomplished, your position is wonderful!

Rooted in Christ, your entire being will be nourished by living water.
You will grow into your true self.
You will blossom forth to do something unique.

     You will love.

Patient's prayer

On my woman
where her trunk
splits into her legs,
there is an opening
which opens out into the universe.

Soon I will enter her cosmos,
and send a message--
a plea for a son--
into the void
and hope
that one day
my prayer will come back from eternity
to wriggle
and cry in my arms.

Doctor-Patient relationship

Vividly distinct,
Her desert over which my consciousness gazes
Stretches into vast interior space.

On the plain thousands of horses lie dead.
Some are beheaded.
All are eviscerated.
Heat emanates from cut-open stomachs in smoking mist.

"This is the world of which I am tired," sighs Polly.
"The world in which I do not live."

She feels empty.
She is anhedonic.
Tar clogs her veins.
She is anorexic.
Sleep eludes her.
The pharmaceutical industry killed her mitochondrial DNA.
Any decision is wrong.
Furies punish her for uncommitted crimes.
All roads lead to more exhausting roads.

After talking a long time,
I hand her the old canteen.

She puts it to her lips.
"No water," she whispers dryly,
And smiles at me with pity.

The narcissist in winter

In the midst of this fury of changing fortunes, the bishop had a falling out with his long-term mistress, Margot Van Buren. When she learned that her hero had become dissatisfied with her recent weight gain and had spent a weekend "spiritually advising" a young triathlete from a Seven Sisters college, Ms. Van Buren grabbed her laptop and marched into the State Attorney General's Office. For immunity, she turned state's witness. She also gave several damning interviews to Dan Truth, an important religion journalist who followed Ladysmith-Jones and the Reformed Catholic Movement. The interviews depicted Ladysmith-Jones as self-deluded, a con man, and a fraud. Of Bishop Ladysmith-Jones's reaction, a *Faith Cathedral* intern said the following:

> When Ms. Van Buren gave her interview, the bishop lost it. Against the advice of everyone, he went on TV and excommunicated Ms. Van Buren. It was so bizarre that the media coverage proliferated into a circus. Story after story about his crimes came out. The Bishop could not manage the damage to his office and ministry. I think he turned to heavy drinking, but this only fueled his erratic behavior. In his public rants, he accused lots of people of disloyalty and heresy and anti-Christian conspiracies. He insisted God would get them. And he kept proclaiming that he represented the authentic soul of the Western world. He looked desperate and silly, declaring holy war against—well, everybody—while insisting on his virtue and importance.

The above observation of the Bishop's behavior under duress is not inconsistent with the narcissistic coping style under pressure. In a study of narcissism and the use of fantasy, Raskin and Novacek (1991) found:

...narcissists cope with stressful experiences by imagining themselves in more ideal situations. In particular, narcissistic persons who are experiencing higher levels of daily stress tend to experience (1) power and revenge fantasies in which they see themselves in a powerful position able to impose punishment on those who have wronged them, and (2) self-admiration fantasies in which they imagine themselves and others admiring their fine qualities of competence, consideration, wisdom, greatness and attractiveness.[2]

Bishop Ladysmith-Jones was suddenly in immense trouble. His public airing of revenge and self-admiration fantasies did not help his reality testing. Several teams of attorneys wanted him to keep a low profile and adhere to sensible legal strategies. Heated arguments ensued and the Bishop fired several excellent, incredulous teams of top legal advisors. One attorney put it this way:

> Whenever we discussed with the Bishop the realities of his legal disadvantages, he either embarked on violent declamations that devolved into rambling non sequiturs, or he accused us of not being for him, so we were against him. Eventually he fired us, which was remarkably stupid, because we're among the profession's best, and we really could have helped him—not to escape reality, which he apparently wanted—but to get a very good deal.

Two events precipitated Bishop Ladysmith-Jones's suicide. First, he rushed unprepared to a deposition with the attorneys working on behalf of a furious parishioner's civil suit. Meticulously prepared, the plaintiff's side asked questions to which they already knew answers. Besides appearing arrogant and hung over, the bishop answered several questions

---

2 Raskin, R. and Novacek, J. (1991). Narcissism and the use of fantasy. *Journal of Clinical Psychology*, 47, (4): 490-499.

in such manner that his perjury was obvious. Secondly, the religion journalist Dan Truth invited Bishop Ladysmith-Jones to participate in an interview to rebut the interview given by his estranged and excommunicated mistress. Ladysmith-Jones made the mistake of allowing Mr. Truth to film the interview. Once released, the video offered audiences an exhausted, furious man incapable of providing clear answers to reasonable questions. Dan Truth said:

> I gave him ample opportunity to clear himself. Why wasn't he a hate monger? Was he having an extramarital affair? Was he a serial cyber stalker? Did he embezzle designated donations? Did he kidnap a rival cleric and force neurotoxic drugs upon the wretch? Was it false that he purchased his bishop's ordination from the Archbishop of London? Et cetera. If there were reasonable explanations, Bishop Ladysmith-Jones did not provide them. He ranted, alluded to enemies and emanated fury. Then he referred to himself as the Reformed Catholic Prophet to the Sacramental Communions of Christendom. That was quite a big title for a very naughty boy to give himself. Ladysmith-Jones was a cartoon. My readers laughed him off the web.

As noted in the introduction of this psychological autopsy, Bishop Ladysmith-Jones left the interview, returned to his rectory, adorned himself in his vestments, prepared documents, drank communion wine, and shot himself in the head. Authorities reported that the final thing that Ladysmith-Jones wrote about himself was that he was a martyr "who died for an unutterably beautiful vision of what the world could be."

On a final forensic note, blood spatter evidence on an open comic book in the rectory study indicated that Ladysmith-

Jones was reading from a section of a Superman comic at some point prior to his suicide.[3]

---

3 Excerpted from Charles Zeiders (2016). A 'psychological autopsy' of a malignant narcissist in church leadership: a composite scenario with discussion. *Journal of Christian Healing*, 3 (1), pp. 1 -29.

The spiritual circumstance of Ned's madness

Prelude

Ned writes to Freud

Dear Chris,

I really wish you had not sent me the *Tommy* CD. The "wicked Uncle Ernie" lyrics upset me immensely. Since Tuesday I've been insomniac and I shake all the time. It feels like every terrible thing that has ever happened to me has concentrated into a demonic emotional valence that saturates me with dread. Pray for me, poet.

Ned

i. Christopher Freud hears Ned's confession

"Having no identity, the result of projects to avoid pain, I belong to no one, not even myself. I am not wise, not serene mystic, nor poet, nor beat poet, nor wild man, nor Russian dancer, nor any other thing known to human eyes. What is most real about me are these headaches, the churning stomach, and the frightened response to others' thoughts about me. These have no merit, nor truth. And the truth is that I am sick with fear and fear death and fear some central obscenity about myself.

"Within me lurks the doubt, the unholy terror that I am unwholesome, centrally flawed, totally failed, impotent, inconsequential, learning disabled, sexually irrelevant, rubber-hooded Pathetico, stinking in sulfurous farts and failures that sweat out shame from putrid glands that stink like carrion meat and Mother's perfume.

"Within me the ghostly dicks of child molesters haunt mouth and anus and stomach and mind and dreams and cognition and blood and act as the spirit of anti-Christ producing obscene consumptive fires that rob the natural vigor from the balls and wilt the dick and stifle laughter and—"

Freud prescribes

> I say dip more tobacco
> And do not be shy with wine
> > nor stingy with caffeine
> > which speeds the mind from its truths
> And pray that God will descend into hell
> Because hell needs the most work.

"Within me the baby buried under laurel by my sister exacts its punishment and kids laugh when I strike out and my tutor beats me and I expect it and may be a masochist which is disgusting and my cousin tricks me and the old guy at the fire house wants to blow me and sends secret vibes into me and my dream uncle does evils and I can't get asylum from my aunt while spontaneously dismembering."

Freud prays for Ned, invoking grace

> Lord have mercy,
> Christ have mercy,
> Lord have mercy.

"Within me skeletons groan under bushes and ferns dance in the breeze and butterflies quiver on corn tips and rabbits launch into hopping and angels laugh and kindness shimmers in the sunlight where girls in cotton dresses sit waiting for me.

"I cannot come to them yet. The locksmith is fashioning a key from silver. It is late and the messenger is apologetic. My heart

sinks and I fight nostalgic impulses. I do not want sentiment.
I want results—results that quiet the strange noises of my
wounded soul. What voice speaks above the noise? Whisper-
ing ministrations whose medicine is hope and love and self-
love and all vehicles of love, like bread and wine, and one
prayerful Freud who is regular and impressive."

Freud prays again, thusly

> Lord Jesus Christ,
> Risen Son of God,
> Have mercy on Ned.

"Hell does not come to me to remain in me.
Hell is a strategic event,
A tactic the Great General uses.
Suffering is the causalty in the war of resurrection.
And, though necessary, my psychological death is another
name for what is not the will of God.
Here is the will of God:

> That I should be self-confident.

> That I should be able to concentrate.
> That I should lie in the arms of my beloved and
>   enjoy the arms of my beloved.
> That I should master a craft.
> That the ghosts of my soul should be laid to rest or
>   redeemed or made into joy.
> That friendship with self should come to pass.
> That friendship without paranoid anxiety and fear of
>   betrayal should find full life in me.
> That my libido should make love to my heart.

> That I should become a man and a good man
>   and not be ashamed in this land,

nor fear to walk in it,
nor apologize for walking in it
nor feel like a stranger in this land,
but know that this land is promised to me
and belongs to me,
and the brooks in this land
I will drink from them.
I will drink from them."

ii. Christopher Freud's intercession

"O Holy God, this day Ned, thy tortured psalmist,
    has confessed of himself unto me.
Within mine own heart have I prayed for thy undoing
    of his undoing,
Conducting an abundance of thy grace to propel him
    toward healings of depth.
But, my Dad and my God,
    Ned needs more of the same.

Please look with kindness upon thy servant
that his disrupted limbic system might enjoy
    thy divine emotions.
That his dis-membering memories might develop
    the re-membering qualities of thy celestial cortex.
That his pathological self-image might enter into
    the Image of God in which it is made.

And may you send angels and archangels unto Ned,
    O Holy Physician,
To protect him from all future harm
    until that time when you invite him
    unto that heavenly café
Wherein thy holy spirits serve mugs of living water
    which is thy Son our Savior, Jesus Christ,

Whose sacrifice makes it highly unlikely
    that You will do anything
    other than to heal Ned into that strong,
    happy creature you designed him to be in the first place.
                                   Amen."

iii. A message to Christopher Freud from Ned's Aunt

Dear Mr. Freud,

While appreciative of your well-meaning association with my nephew Ned, and further appreciative of your enthusiasm for the idea that certain religious practices derived from the traditions of orthodox Christianity can bring about positive psychological shifts in those diagnosed as mentally disturbed, we—that is Ned's Uncle and myself—respectfully ask you to immediately desist from any further association with Ned, including letters or phone communications. We request this for two reasons: 1) As a poet, Ned is highly imaginative and unfortunately prone to evade responsibility for his problems by escaping into fantasy, 2) Experts who are perhaps less "enthusiastic" and more informed about alleviating mental illness than yourself have invited Ned's uncle and myself—who presently hold power of attorney—to enroll Ned in a program designed to treat his problems using empirically tested pharmaceuticals. If you interfere with Ned's welfare by failing to comply with our request, Mr. Freud, we will seek a restraining order before suing you for damages.

Sincerely yours,
Ned's Aunt

iv. Shortly into his new treatment, Ned hears a voice

I put my lips to your forehead
    and sing my songs to your limbic system.

Your neurons learn my hymns;
> in your occipital lobe
> visions of angels dance before the eyes of your mind.

I give you a ministry to yourself.
You reach to your fragments and embrace them like sons.
You hold yourself and dance.

Here is my grace:
> that you have parts but are whole,
> that you yearn without wanting
> that you give but gain from expending.

I have sung myself to yourself;
> into the cells of your body have I sung myself
> and shown you the truth
> which is that you are like me,
> as I am the One who sends me to you.

v. The horror and judgment of Ned's wicked Uncle

Ned's Uncle never spoke of what took place between himself and his nephew so many years ago. He terrified himself by recalling the softness of the August evening and the smell of the meadow grass as he set the boy down amid the fragrant straw. He closed his eyes and snuggled to the child and breathed in his skin and in a shuddering instant, set forth the future of another man's agony.

In the burning air, just out of Uncle's mind, infuriated spirits fashioned a millstone and the sea exploded before the merciless Judge on the indignant throne. There was silence and then a great work needed to be done.[4]

---

4 Parts of this long poem were published in excerpts in *Wall Street Revolution and Other Poems* by *il piccolo editions* (2013).

vi. Ned's Uncle in hell (Christopher Freud's dream)

Deprived of the vision of God, in the location of the damned, Ned's Uncle must ever read aloud his indictment:

> "Rape is the forcible violation of the sexual intimacy of another person. It does injury to justice and charity. Rape deeply wounds the respect, freedom, and physical and moral integrity to which every person has a right. It causes grave damage which can mark the victim for life. It is always an intrinsically evil act. Graver still is the rape of children committed by parents (incest) or those responsible for the education of the children entrusted to them."[5]

A mob listens, gazes, grotesquely fascinated and incensed. A sickened spokesman howls,

"Repulsion and grief for your condition spreads from eye to heart
And years shall pass before this horror fades.[6]

"From sickness at your sight
I would evacuate your visage,
But my dead spirit can
Neither vomit nor shit
As do the bodies of the living."

Amid the din and stench, dirty cameras on tripods record it all.

Detesting eyes comprehend the pederast.
Here is the anguishing element of his punishment:

5 Catholic Church. (1994). *Catechism of the Catholic Church*. New York, NY: Image Books, p. 62.
6 Adapted from Marc Musa (Ed.). (1995). *The Portable Dante*. New York: NY: Penguin Books, p. 86.

To be seen
Accurately in true sin
Is to die endlessly of
Shame.

The butterfly lands

The butterfly lands
    on a small rock in mid-brook.
He spreads wings
    of dark opal
    atop rock mass
    of unfathomable green;

      the slightest breeze from beach grove
      the murmur of stream
      and the tiny antenna moves a fraction.

The trout hovers beside
    the rock in water.
He is still.
He moves a fin

      and in the life-filled hush
      thinks with the butterfly.

POSTLUDE

In a dream I flew above the Schuylkill River

In a dream I flew above the Schuylkill River.
My wings were strong.
Below me ran a pretty athlete.
It was Magdalena the X-ray Technician.
I knew that she was kind,
Because she smelled like chocolate.

I flew
From Valley Forge to Manayunk.
There I saw my patient Cartwright.

He stood atop the steeple
Of St. John the Baptist Church.

The devil was with him.
The devil showed Cartwright
Center City Philadelphia,
The plains of New Jersey,
Atlantic City,
And the Atlantic Ocean;

The ocean was filled with pleasure boats
And bathing beauties.

Plump, amorous Cartwright prepared to
Bow down and worship Nick.
He would deal with the devil.
Power and the pleasure would be given to him, he thought.

But the devil admonished Cartwright.
He explained that he sought to hire someone
With more force of character, more gravitas,
More physical presence, and more charisma.

He sought someone who would
Better represent the brand.

The devil disappeared in smoke. Almost apologetically.

Fat, sniffling Cartwright descended from the tower.
He had a lump in his throat.
On chubby feet soaked with corpulent tears
He reeled to the bank of the river.

By the waters of the Schuylkill
Cartwright lay down and wept.

In the distance Mrs. Porter ascended into heaven.
She rose above the Comcast Building.
She read the Bulletin of the Daughters of the American Revolution.
She vanished in the stratosphere.

At that very moment
Magdalena the X-ray Technician
Jogged near.
She heard the fat man sobbing.
Sweetness in her heart awaited expression.

(She came from nowhere, it seemed,
But there were angels all around.)

She knew without need of developed story
That she and Cartwright would enjoy the glory
Of un-cinematic, real love
Cherished in wholesome obscurity.

She raised Cartwright to his feet.
She did her best.
She opened a little door betwixt her breasts
And revealed a miniscule compartment stuffed with chocolates.

From that moment
Fat Cartwright's countenance brightened
And Magdalena loved him.

"KISS EPIPHANY": A SPIRITUAL CRITIQUE OF *LOVE POEMS AND OTHER TERRIBLE PROBLEMS*

When first viewing Pieter Brueghel's famous work, "The Triumph of Death," one is daunted by the obvious message: the riot of death is omnipresent and irresistible. All is foul carnage. And one can stare at the painting for a long time before spotting the all-important, meaning-making anomaly: two lovers in the bottom right-hand corner who seem unperturbed by the disaster, for they only have eyes (as the old song goes) for one another. This is a bold statement about the nature of eros—its intensity, silliness, and holiness. One immediately considers what their world must look like from within. The first half of Charles Zeiders' new collection of poems, *Love Poems and Other Terrible Problems*, takes us deeply into that world of eros and reverses the picture: the lovers are in the forefront, and the death-in-life carnage is but a muffled sound in the distance.

The volume begins with "A description of things in the tradition of Walt Whitman," when the cool-headed speaker—reveling in his own placidity in a panic-stricken world—is tempted into the realm of abstraction. But he decides to abide in the concrete world, which is where he belongs. His reward for not disdaining the concrete is that he stumbles upon earthly romance and experiences matrimonial love as a Sacrament: "You connect me to the farthest stars in the universe/ And to the ground beneath my feet" ("You"). Thus the speaker is drawn, deeper than he could have imagined, into the mystery of Christ's holy love. In true Gospel fashion, the way up is down. The way to true spirituality is through the humility of sanctified, material things.

What strikes one first about Zeiders' love poems is their instinct for all the paradoxes of a Christ-redeemed eros. For example, the reader has a sense of participation in this particular romance. This is no mere voyeurism; like the guests at a wedding, one is aware of one's office as a witness and at the same time feels the interconnectedness of a Sacrament.

Such paradoxes abound. In poems like "Innocent Freudian poem" and "Seven schmi-ku" the tone is serious but extremely playful. I am reminded of how in The Four Loves, C.S. Lewis insists that to take eros too seriously is to risk becoming an idolater; to fail to recognize its holiness is to risk becoming a base fornicator. So the speaker in Zeiders' love poems is, like all lovers, at once a leonine sex god and a clumsy, silly man.

The second and larger section of the volume—the "other terrible problems"—deals with darker subjects: extreme selfishness, misplaced and misapplied yearnings, and the many other unrealities which fallen humans create. However, we begin this journey into the land of unreality with our heads screwed on right. All Sacrament is a grounding in The Ultimate Reality: "Your gaze and your touch/ Outwardly express/ That Eternity's Author/Has something rather beautiful in mind" ("The sacrament of our joyful invincibility"). This is a solid place to stand if one is going to survey a land of shadow. The earlier sacramental love poems cast light behind them, and the "terrible problems" are exposed for what they are: lack of love, misplaced love, and love-gone-wrong.

While Zeiders creates several captivating voices throughout the collection, perhaps his best (and most affection-inspiring) is "plump, amorous Cartwright." He is perpetually disappointed and nearly despairing, but not despairing enough to free him of his mastering desire for Mrs. Porter, alas! One feels the depth of his loneliness and mental imprisonment. When Mrs. Porter denies him sexual release after some initial petting, he lies in bed beside her:

I was inflamed with lust and hope.
At any moment you would come to your senses
And we would make love.
But we did not make love.
We lay there.
("Cold: Cartwright's second lament")

In wishing to be free from the constraints of Christian sexual morality, Cartwright is enslaved; in the same way, modern secular society, in its refusal to treat sex as sacred, ends up creating an all-consuming idol. The contrast between the first and second section is unmistakable, and having been in the realm of Christ-redeemed eros, one feels Cartwright's folly deeply. Unsanctified love is such a pathetic parody of Christian matrimony that one is overcome by the enormity of the deception.

Like Dante's Virgil, Zeiders navigates us through an earthly Inferno of malignant narcissists, charlatans, and pedophiles. Some of these vignettes expose not only warped or misplaced love, but love that has fallen so far that it is inverted into hate and the spirit of antichrist. Though riveting reading, "The Narcissist in spring," "The Narcissist in winter," and the most chilling portions of "The spiritual circumstance of Ned's madness" are written in prose and suggest the banality of such evil.

Thankfully, the poet brings us safely to the other side. Just as the Christian vision of the universe begins and ends with Love, so *Love Poems and Other Terrible Problems* provides hope. Even in the darkest places, Love sustains and consoles us. The bold voice of the Christian therapist, Christopher Freud, is particularly moving as he speaks to God on behalf of his patients. In "The spiritual circumstance of Ned's madness" he speaks these words of benediction, asking the blessing of Christ,

Whose sacrifice makes it highly unlikely
that You will do anything
other than to heal Ned into that strong,
happy creature you designed him to be in the first place.

Some of the subject matter of this volume might be—and
has been—explored in didactic prose, but like all good poetry,
Love Poems and Other Terrible Problems relates that information
experientially (in a way didactic prose cannot, and in a com-
paratively short number of pages). Although Zeiders is never
guilty of inelegant moralization, this collection has great value
as an antidote for the dull, narrow, and ultimately low moral
imagination of our sexually backward society. In a time when
marriage is thought to be an isolated and private affair, one
experiences connection and the value of a love that is not
one's own. In culture that is convinced only "free" sex is excit-
ing (and love in the bonds of matrimony is dull and stifling),
Zeiders' robust and lusty vision of Sacramental eros may be
something like "a kiss epiphany."

Joseph Walls
Poet
Virginia Bach, VA
January 25, 2017

EDITOR'S AFTERWORD

At the start of this collection of poems by Charles Zeiders, a persona turns away from external "authoritative" voices crying doom and toward the inner voices that must be heeded. These inner voices resist both the chaos and panic of contemporary politics and the escapist invitation to have some "moon port," "a drink."

Taking a stand between those two poles, the speaker settles into what one knows of one's own wisdom:

> Everything is ambiguous and you no longer fear that.
> There are people left alive whom you love.
> You are the man who blessed someone today.
> A secret good thing occurs, but no one knows its nature.

These are the conditions of life: the yin and the yang of what one knows, what one does not know. This is life on life's terms, and the terms of life are accepted. From this strong stance it is possible to catch the updraft of love, to know who one is and whom one should marry: this one.

The *Love Poems* of Part I show us the container of love in which one's entire humanity can be accepted, by oneself and by the other one. In a fancy restaurant, the evening is not going well. Pomposity and insecurity cast their pall. And so

> I feel heartbroken and homesick
> But I do not care.
> In that dress you look lovely.

Or again,

I am embarrassed.
But I love you,
So my embarrassment does not embarrass me.

There is something bigger here than the self-scrutinizing, self-absorbed individual. That larger thing is the couple: but not just any couple, the couple who bless one another with water, who pray, who find the living water in the woods and the spirit blowing where it will, who believe the psalm that says to the Lord "you alone make me dwell in safety."

And so in turn the couple is not self-absorbed, happy in their own cocoon. He goes "off to my practice/ to heal the sick"; she gives her music and her paintings to the world. They also know they are not the only couple in the world, as some love poems might have it. Their rosy glow shines even on the comical Cartwright who has "No luck with Mrs. Porter. None tonight." And by resonance their world includes the love rendered "meticulously" in Wyeth's painting of Helga.

From the exploration of this transfigured state we turn to the *Other Terrible Problems* of Part II. We know this world. This is the world we enter when we come back down from the mountain. Here it is only a leaf that the wind carries upward. Nietzschean nihilism presses upon us. So does war and gore, sometimes in our dreams. Psychopaths head our institutions, and we cannot find a way to offer our eros in the mad contexts they create. Sex becomes farcical – but even so, not funny.

We turn to therapy. Here too we may find a spiritual wasteland. The capacity of the therapist to defend against his own "self-loathing and humiliation" may barely exceed the capacity of the person he is hired to help. Intellectualization takes Narcissus further and further into the loneliness of self; wives and other people vaporize until all that remains is the single self and madness. It is the opposite of what we have seen in the

Love Poems. The spiral spirals only centripetally, and never reaches the heart.

Because he is a psychotherapist as well as a poet, Dr. Charles Zeiders is well positioned to render a portrait of our times. In this collection he invokes the precedent of Whitman, who—a Civil War nurse as well as a poet—delineated a nation and the characteristics of the "representative men" who formed it: on the one hand expanding, confident, democratic; on the other, a nation tearing itself apart. Eros (of course) impelled Whitman's creativity, just as eros impels Zeiders' "Love Poems." And eros led Whitman to attend the wounded on America's battlefields, just as eros underlies the psychotherapist's desire to heal and his ability to endure the complexities and limitations of that vocation.

What is the verbal construct that makes possible this portrait of America still in the early part of the twenty-first century, this era characterized by so much therapy and so much need for it? In a Whitmanesque style, Zeiders' lines are conversational and irregular in length. Much of the language is of an easy everyday nature. Three or four strong beats a line often give these poems their shapeliness, but so do repetition ("Our love … Our love … Our love"; or "Like … Like… Like") and the consolidations marked by the occasional use of rhyme. Some particularly striking rhymes are "gem / HaShem" and "undressed / unimpressed." Like Whitman naming the native plants among his leaves of grass, Zeiders enjoys the specificity of "fiddleheads" and "sycamore," and the sound of these words.

Most empowering, however, is Zeiders' adoption of various voices, and here he departs somewhat from Whitman, who, even if he was large and did contain multitudes, was not much given to creating personas through whom to speak.

With Zeiders, however, we have a cast of characters that has developed over time from one collection to the next: the lamentable and lamenting Cartwright; the professional cohort of Christopher Freud, Dr. Zingfeld, and Sarah Sue Wong; the emeritus professor Jacques Foucault who cuts to shreds the ambitions of "Mr. Writer Guy." At times Zeiders deliberately has his characters reveal themselves in awkward language, as in Cartwright's "Coital magnificence will be ours, you sweetie!" or in the prayer in which Christopher Freud stumbles from one level of diction to another in an attempt to address God on behalf of his patient. Nor is Zeiders afraid to embrace even prose in this collection, whether quoting from his own professional articles or from the *Catechism of the Catholic Church*.

What else but a multi-voiced and multivalent chorus would be adequate to the times in which we live, in which there is no "Unitary Self" or "Text of Absolute Meaning" such as (we think) there used to be? Go, little book: charm, tease, provoke; uplift, confront, and make us laugh and give us strength to carry on.

Margaret Connolly
Editor
Philadelphia, PA
January 15, 2017

Acknowledgments

I extend heartfelt thanks to Dr. Christine Jackson, Todd Lesh, and Samantha Schwartz for their invaluable editorial assistance and artistic ministrations. Thanks also to brilliant Selvin Glass (www.selvinglass.com) for generating the "Mysterious Muse" for the cover. Most of all I am grateful to those who have welcomed me into their stories. The secret Jerusalem awaits when the work gets done.

Contributors

Peter Devlin is a writer residing in Washington D.C. He received his B.A. from the University of Pennsylvania and his M.S.W. from the Suzanne Dworak-Peck School of Social Work at the University of Southern California.

Joseph Walls holds a Master of Arts in English from Liberty University. His award-winning thesis, *A Hierarchy of Love: Myth in C.S. Lewis' Perelandra*, investigates the connection between Lewis' understanding of mythos and depiction of Sacrament. Joseph lives with his family in Virginia Beach, where he teaches English at a local community college and soaks in the sacramental grace of the natural world.

Margaret Connolly earned her PhD in English at Stanford University and has taught at New York University and Villanova University. She is a specialist in Virginia Woolf, and has published work on Woolf's anti-fascism.

il piccolo editions is an imprint of Fisher King Enterprises.
Learn more about many other worthy publications at:
www.fisherkingpress.com

Made in the USA
Middletown, DE
09 June 2023